The Haunting of My Thoughts

A collection of poetry

by:
Unique Waterfall

Published by: Unique Waterfall through Kindle Direct Publishing

Edited by: Shades of Soul Productions

Cover design by: H.Shay

Email the author: Unique_Waterfall@yahoo.com

Below ISBN refers to print edition:

978-0-9882943-3-2

III. *Truth*

IV. *Love*

Introduction

Writing is my life. It has been my shelter, my outlet, and my solace. I want to welcome you to my....

CHAOS

Words rambling
Thoughts scattered
Don't know what to do
So confused
Who are you
Issues have found me
Won't let me be
They just keep screaming

Please leave me alone
Can't find my way home
A pen some paper
My refuse you see
Have to write it all down
Get it out of me
Won't cease until I do
Will I make it through

This next or the next
All I want is some rest
Won't get it now
I have to somehow
Quiet my mind
Slowly with time
It ask starts to cease
This beast within me

I now have some peace
Praying she doesn't break free....

LIFE...

Life

BY THE WAY

Chasing these words ain't easy you see
You gotta know how to put them down lyrically
If you don't know how to do it, then have a seat
Watch the master work these words fluently
It's like when we make love when I'm done it's my masterpiece

Intertwining, unwinding, to strapping and grabbing
The words flow from my mouth like your orgasm
Flowing and pouring it out you become numb
Maybe it's the way I use my tongue

It doesn't matter which way
Whether I'm licking or spitting these words to you
I'm going to make sure you're satisfied it's what I do
I'm just trying to give you a taste
A taste of how these words will have you dazed

I'm sorry, I didn't tell you my name
Didn't mean to give it to you all that way
Especially since I just met you today
But just like these words
You all over me

Got me pantin and sweatin
A challenge for me –Naw
Overwhelming it becomes when you need to cum
Wait it's on the tip of my tongue
Damn girl what cha doing to me

The end of the round
It's finna go down
I hope you don't mind me going deep
Deep with these words you've just heard
Thrust into your spirit

Tell me Ma I know you feel it
It was great to meet you
Can we do this again next week?
Oh, by the way my name is Unique!

Life

OVERCOME

What I need is simple you see

Direction is what I seek

Failure seems to keep following me

Tired of not being who I was created to be

The greatest in the world is what I should be

Things keep tearing me down

Don't want to be this way

Please Lord help me I pray

Just when I think I've figured it out

Bam there it is without a doubt

Failure that thing that I hate

Won't allow you to take control

Whatever it takes I'm going to make it right

Don't' wanna live a lie

Giving failure back this negative sight

I'm claiming Victory

Cause that's the way it should be

I'm Victorious because that's the way THE CREATOR MADE ME

Failure is no longer an option

Nor is he in sight in my life!

3

Life

OLOW

OLOW
FIRST THING IN THE MORNING I SAY TO YOU....

OLOW
THROUGH OUT THE DAY FOR YOU SEEING ME THROUGH...

OLOW
BECAUSE THERE IS NO ME WITHOUT YOU...

OLOW
FOR HELPING MY SITUATIONS CHANGE....

OLOW
FOR THE LOVE YOU HAVE FOR ME.....

OLOW
MY DAY IS NOW COMPLETE....

OLOW
FOR WATCHING OVER ME WHILE I SLEEP....

OLOW
FOR YOUR GRACE AND MERCY....

OLOW
FOR ALL THAT YOU'VE DONE FOR ME....

OLOW!!!

Life

MEMORY

When I'm gone will you remember me
Remember what it was like to talk to me
The curve my mouth made when you made me angry
What about the joy I screamed out when the lord awakened me

When I'm gone will you remember me
The million and one question I asked that made me happy
Cartoons on the TV because it was all I wanted to see
That meal I fixed that had you saying ooh wee

When I'm gone will you remember me
All the hard work I did untiredly
Late nights up with no sleep working my ass off completely
Accomplishing a great deed trying to be a better human being

When I gone will you remember me
Those late-night cries me asking why
Why did this have to happen to me
Oh Lord please take this fate from me

When I gone will you remember me
The good times the worst times all just memories
So grateful for how much you were a friend to me
A lasting love that I will take with me

When I'm gone don't shed a tear
Remember what drew us near
What you have of me stored in your heart
Means we will never be far apart
Please remember me…

Life

MY NAME

What you call me
Shorty, baby girl, damn with your thick azz
Excuse me?
That's not my name!

I understand you see all this beauty
And you think it's your duty to approach
But let's get one thing clear

I'm not your baby girl, shorty, or thick azz
My name is Queen!
Address me as such
Don't get it twisted

I can become your thick azz baby girl
Shorty!
But come correct or not at all
Cause you see I need more than just that tired line

I was once a baby girl
Never a shorty
But now a thick azz woman...

Life

SOVEREIGNTY

I'm from another world
Will never conform to these restrictions
Free as a bird don't care who's concern
A spirit so enormous it longs to be free
Dancing by the way side
Twirling my imagination
I live within my reality
Your standards I don't understand
Why conform to blend and bend
I'll rather be judged for what I believe in
A spirit so beautiful it longs to be free
Not a care in the world
Because I now finally accept me!
Sovereignty...

Life

IGNORANCE

LOOK BEYOND THAT TITLE YOU GAVE
TO TRY AN REDUCE ME
NO YOU MAY NOT
FOR I AM A HUMAN JUST LIKE YOU
WHERE IS YOUR TITLE
YOU HOLD NONE
I DON'T ACCEPT THAT
BUT YOU FEEL THE NEED TO LABEL ME
I WILL NOT LET YOU DEFINE WHO I AM
FOR I AM A HUMAN JUST LIKE YOU
A WOMAN OF MANY TALENTS
BUT YOU CAN'T SEE
I KNOW WHO I AM AND WHAT'S INSIDE ME
A SURVIVOR
A MOTHER
A FRIEND
A LOVER
A PERSON WITH ENORMOUS STRENGTH
NOT THE UGLY THINGS YOU THROW OUT
THE HATE THAT LIES WITHIN YOUR HEART

Life

RELIEF

I heard about you
Can you really make my dreams come true
I've been searching for someone to
Do you really think it could be you
I tried so many others
But they let me down
Much disappointment for me
So you tell me how you're different, exactly
Look how small you are
I've had bigger
Wasn't any better though
Let me look at you a little more closely
Wouldn't want my eyes to deceive me
You say after an hour I'll be dreaming
Ok let me get ready
So anxious to try you out
Pour me some water her goes
I insert you in my mouth and swallow
You go down so smooth
Waiting for the magic that you promised me
Oh, I'm feeling it now
I'm getting sleepy
I lay my head down faithfully still
You were right I'm dreaming now
My new sleeping pill...

Life

MY LIFE

I'm an Alien in this strange place
No where do I fit in or belong
My thoughts light years ahead
Never following the crowd
Always standing alone
What I love is frowned upon
Does that change me
Hell no
Makes me stronger
Helps me grow
Never trading me
Accepting my weird
Embracing my beauty
UNIQUE!

Life

CONTEMPT

offended many
took away our self esteem
along with our dignity
now you toss it around like it doesn't sting

yet it does pierce to the core
I don't want to hear the word no more
remove it from your VERNACULAR
chose something else to call

your guy
your boy
your ace
not that word it's a disgrace!

MY N!&&@

PASSION...

Passion

IT IS SHE....

How do you go from Phucking me to making love to me
all in a matter of hours

How is it that you can take my body to such places that I
never image

I beg, I scream, I moan, I cry out in ecstasy please, no,
stop, don't!

But as the time goes we float closer and closer to that
breaking point

I tremble, you shake, I quiver, you rock

Closer, Closer, Closer my body calls out for that touch
that moment like no other

Bam, Damn it's here please, no, oh, yes, oh, wow, damn!

You've done more than I ever could image

You've taken it to a level that can't be touched

Oh why, oh why, don't give it to me in this way please,
no, stop, don't!

Too late, my juice, your juice, our juice aroma fills the air

Can't catch my breath, don't want it to end, please rewind

Can't get you out my mind, off my skin, out my heart

That night, this night, all the other nights, how, why, only
you

How is it possible?
Tell me...

13

Passion

FEELINGS

I love you with all that I am
I give you all of me in every way
You are my air to breath
Emotions high for you
Need you to know that
Every waking moment spent I think of you
Didn't know someone could have this kind of effect
Don't recognize this feeling
Sweating palms
Beating heart
Speechless when you come around
What to do I don't have a clue
How can I feel this way
Is this ok
Must tell you don't know how
You alone have my heart
Must break free
Never before has anyone taken over me the way you do
Ready to give in here goes
Going to let you know
I've fallen and fallen hard
I love a woman!!!

Passion

BOND

Looking out across the room
I see a face bright as the moon
Your radiance draws me in
My life won't be the same again
The electrifying pull that is your being
Has taken a hold of me
A grip so strong it has me weak
Tell me please how can this be
Another soul to penetrate me
With just one look and not physically
You have locked in on my mental
I beg of you please be gentle
My weakness you have now found
Stroking my thoughts
Planting the seeds that is you
Creating a bond that only you and I share
The only one who holds my heart near.....

Passion

PILLAR

I NEED YOU TO KNOW
THAT WHEN YOU ARE DOWN
I'LL BE THAT ENERGY THAT UPLIFTS YOU
WHEN LIFE GETS HARD
I'LL BE YOUR RELIEF
IF YOU EVER CRY
YOUR TEARS I'LL WIPE AWAY
YOU'LL NEVER BE INSECURE
FOR I AM YOUR SECURITY FOR ALWAYS
I DON'T KNOW WHAT TRAILS THIS WORLD MAY BRING
BUT FOREVER I AM BY YOUR SIDE
NO MATTER THE TURBULENCE...

Passion

BLUE

A walk on the beach
The oceans blue
The calm wave rolling by
A beautiful night
Such a pleasant delight to become one
The sand between my toes
The nature that is love
Thinking of you and only you
The one whom has my heart
The sounds of the night quickly take me over
Nothing more beautiful than the rich color of black satin across the sky
Star's sparking brightly
The whistling of the breeze
Your scent in my nose
Wish you were near
Close my eyes to imprint this night that reminds me of you
A memory that will always be of my true love

Passion

REMNANTS

I close my eyes
Remnants of you dance on my skin
Wishing I could relive last night again
The way you caressed my flesh
But penetrated my soul
No words can utter
The pleasure that unfolded
Both our bodies
Being taking to the extreme
Damn girl this is ecstasy
Turning me on to new possible things
Please tell me this is not a dream!
For I never want to awaken
From your magic touch
The center of my universe
Is now only yours to please
All I ask of you now is just be
Gentle with me

Passion

MERGED

My 2 loves merged as 1
What a dream come true
My hands in Euphoria
Touching both of you

The art of your body
Brings out the music in me
Rhythm and notes flow
Phenomenally....

Caressing your figure
Making mad beats
The sound of your moans are
Electrifying....

The harder I play
The better it gets
Bringing us closer to
Climax....

Don't want this to end
The beautiful love we just made
Our song forever
Will continue to play

Passion

TWIN FLAME

Laying watching perfection that is you
Your skin glistening
My flesh itching
Licking my lips
Waiting for the moment

My essence
Your vessel
Becomes our aroma
A sweet delight
A cosmic experience we will share

In a trance for you are my heaven
My deliverance
Your existence has me under a spell
For which I never want to recover
A dare a moment in time

You've finally arrived
This is our destiny
Time to make history
Write our story in the sky
Closer, we are now becoming one

This spiritual exchange of human flesh
I've lost my breath it is yours now
Your vessel taking my essence
Manifesting into the best creation
Energy that cannot be tamed

Centered around the universe
A galaxy that is only ours
Drifting among the stars
It is you my one and only
Twin flame...

Passion

FANTASY

Day dreaming thinking of you wishing we could be near
You are so far away I can only be close to you when I close my eyes
I image what you are doing wish that I could see
Tell me do you also miss me

I often close my eyes to fantasize about you and I
To smell your scent to touch your skin
Butterflies all in my stomach watching the clock
Can't wait until I'm sleep again

I see you in my dreams smiling back at me
Longing for the same your sweet kisses I miss
Please keep me company as long as you can
For I don't want to awake from this

You are my best kept secret and I am yours
What we are sharing they won't understand
For I am yours and you are mine
But only in dream land

Passion

UNFAMILIAR

You are all in my mental
Invading my space with your presence
An unfamiliar feeling has taken hold of me
Close my eyes it's your face I see
Your smile warms my soul
My heart pounds whenever you're around
Sweaty palm and butterflies
You make me tongue tied
Unable to articulate my thoughts
For they are all about you
What has come over me
This is foreign to my brain
I don't understand
Not really trying to
I want fate to take control
Us becoming what I dream
Time will tell if it's meant to be
 You and I will turn into
WE...

Passion

PASSION

I'm dangerous

I'm deadly

Not how you think

But hey maybe

The feelings I'll inflict

My love is deep

It penetrates beyond the surface

Digs deep into the pit of your core

Your souls not safe

I tried to warn you

Be ready for this

I will fuck up your existence

The emotions I make you feel

Having you screaming

Why me!

Intoxicating realm you can't emerge from

I have you

My victim

My conquest

My love....

Is dangerous!

Passion

AMOUR

I can taste your body in my sleep
Got me feenin after thee
Your nectar so sweet
Can't wait to devour your treat
Turn around let me gaze upon your beauty
Take you into my hands
The beginning of love
The taste of skin tingles my lips
The thickness of your sap filling my throat
Drinking down your essence
The exit of ecstasy
Giving me life
Ounce by ounce
Satisfying my crave
Head back
Toes curled
Pleasing you as you deserve
Time for the finale
Don't hold back
Just hold on and release that.......
Umm, sweet essence of you

TRUTH...

Truth

RIPPED

Dear heart you don't beat anymore
Could it be because of the pain you bore
Torn apart by someone you loved
It hurts so deep didn't know that it could
Just want this pain to stop right now
Don't know when I will ever be whole

Now she's sorry for what she did
What to do with those words
Do I even believe them
No I don't think I do
The pain is just unbearable

This pain I bare won't let me forgive
Forgive you for what you caused
My dreams our plans the perfect family
All gone away
My life changed in just one day

You didn't have to do this to me
To us you broke our trust
For what!
Was it worth my heart
Hell No it wasn't

But the lesson here is
You don't deserve me
Picking up the pieces that is my life
Know that it's ok
That I still love you
But never again will you get the chance to hurt me

Thank you for showing me who you truly are
You can keep your lies and your deceit
Will forgive you for my own peace
I'm moving on from you
No more contact I wish you luck
I was the best thing in your life
But you fucked that up!

Truth

FATAL

What have you done
What have I done
This couldn't be

You made me do this to you
Why ooh Why you didn't have to lie
How could you

I thought you would be true
I should have known you were fatal
Only for a little while did I have you

It's warm in here but yet you are cold
I tried to hold you, but it was too late
I didn't mean to, but you made me

I dropped it covered with your love
So, the love I thought but it was actually blood
I am sorry it wasn't you who was fatal

It turned out that your deceit is what made
Me this love our so call love
Fatal!

Truth
FREE TO

I'm free to love whom I want

You can't judge me

Fuck the naysayer

Have you experienced it

The chemical intoxicating powerful love that two women share

You will never understand

You have to experience it to know

Don't knock it unless you tried it

And if you tried it then you know

To be loved by a woman is like no other

I wouldn't trade it for the world

Not my girl

Will love her to the end of time

Don't try to take that away

We will fight for this

It's who we are what we stand for

No one not you or anyone else can change that

LESBIAN LOVE IS POWERFUL

Truth

Painful

It hurts its painful this feeling inside I can no longer bear
I wonder what will happen if I dare to share
Don't know what to do or how to act
Just keep my mouth close
If my secret gets out I am sure to lose
My family my friends those whom care
No one understands oh how I don't want to be with a man

Must keep a straight face no time for truth
That is if they see me staring at you
The women I love this feeling I can't share
How long can I keep this inside or do I dare
The bad things that will happen if I stand up tall
No longer a fake but to thine self being true
The whispers the faces the good mornings no more

Now my secret is out don't know what to do
Please help me make it without being blue
How do I face the people I love
No questions just listen it's not your fault
My creator made me this way without a doubt
Say what you wish think what you may
This is my life and I am going to live it my way

NO longer ashamed afraid or in hiding
You only live once can you please just stand beside me
I need your support and also your love
I'm still the same person as I was before
Nothing has changed about little old me
Just the love I have to give is not for a he
You don't understand how painful it is

To be told that you're different all cause of fear
Can be beaten and bruised for loving the same
My goodness people do you have no shame
What is it to you whom I choose to love
I'm not hurting anyone
I only have to answer to the one above
Please leave me be find you some business

This is my life now please let me live it......

Truth

DECISIONS

If I bought you the world because I wanted you to be my girl
Will you say yes or no

If I told you I didn't love you what would you do
Could you make me fall back in love with you

If I was unfaithful would you leave me all alone
Would you try to make it work or just walk away

If I made you cry would you turn your head from me
Or would you allow me to wipe away your tears

What if whenever you call I never picked up the phone
Would you stop trying to call

If I slapped you and said I love you
Would you think it was true

When you came around I treated you like you were nothing
Would you walk out my life

What if I said all the things I've done to you is because I am a fool
Would you stay and stand this test at hand
Or will you wash your hands and make it the end

Because no matter what
You are worth more than

Being slapped, made cry, unfaithfulness, unloved, and ignored

Truth

MINUTE

A minute can change anything
A minute can change everything
One minute you're happy
One minute you're sad
The next minute you're mad
Don't know what to do
Things seem all cool
Then the next minute I'm bugging you
Don't spend any time
All I hear is whining
I don't do this
I don't do that
WHY WHY WHY
CRY CRY CRY
One minute can change a whole lot of things
In one minute you can become mean
One minute you're the best in the whole world
The next minute you don't want to be my girl
So dark and depressed is the mood from you
No matter if I say I love you
One minute we can be the perfect family
The next minute you're saying you're leaving me
Don't know when you're happy only when you're sad
Pretending to be
Make is seem like everything is cool
But actually I' m the one who's the fool
Foolish enough to think this was supposed to be
But now my minute is up
The curtain has come down
One thing is for certain
A minute can change
You for a life time

TRUTH

The relationship is over
It is my fault
I don't know why I continue to cry
Cry for something
That has not been true
But baby for what it's worth
I DID LOVE YOU
Can you really say
That I was your heart
What was really your angle
From the start
Now that it's over
We have both moved on
We now only have memories
Of the love that has gone

Truth

REJECT

I've tried to love you
With all that's in me
But all you've done is reject me
How long do you think this will be
Do I walk out the door for you to see
What you have standing before you
In me
Someone who will move mountains
To fulfill your desires
Will plead to heaven to make your
Dreams come true
Sad part is all this
I'll do for you
When you can't be true
Busy worried about the wrong thing
Instead of just loving me
But now I realized I must move on
To bigger and brighter things
So carry on
I hope you find
What you didn't see in me
That was a woman who loved you
Unconditionally

Truth
TRACES

I think of you often
Traces of our past
That first moment that changed my heart
That decision that broke yours
We can't go back
I still remember your touch
Scared to give in
You tried to free me
But I wasn't ready
Please forgive me
You loved me
I used you
That final moment
Nothing but pain in your eyes
Forever in my heart
That piece of you
For you changed my life
If only I could tell you
I think of you often....

Truth
PIECES

I'm broken
I'm not perfect
Delicate
About to fall apart
Don't know where to start
Picking up the pieces
That is my life
Will this hurt subside
Or even pass
So many years with you
Now my first hour without you
How do I go on
Eyes heavy hiding the shame
Gave you all within me
Blurred vision wouldn't let me see
It never was meant to be
Alone totally
No good for the next inline
Will happiness ever come into my life
Don't know how long that will be
Hope someone will take a chance on me
Picking up the pieces
That is my life

Truth

CONFORM

I'm from another world
Will never conform to these restrictions
Free as a bird
Don't care who's concern
A spirit so enormous it longs to be free
Dancing by the way side
Twirling my imagination
I live within my reality
Your standards I don't understand
Why conform to blend
I'll rather be judged for what I believe in
A spirit so beautiful it has to be freed
Not a care in the world
Because I now finally accept me!

TRUST

when your heart is broken
what's the point of mending it
trusting in you
lead to this series
me being let down
a great beginning
but a difficult end
no longer the person I knew
lost myself trying to find you
holding on to memories
slowly fading reality
not what it used to be
feeling ways I never image
pit of my stomach aching with anger
still loving you no matter what
can't turn off these feelings
just want to cut out our reality
Things just couldn't be....

LOVE...

Love

EVER

Spread your legs open wide
I'm dying to be inside
Feeling your warmth, I want to go deep

Girl don't keep it from me
Your love hole is calling I want to be the one
Giving you all that you need

Baby give it to me boo please
Don't tease me give me what I ask
I promise you will enjoy it

Please let me get inside
I want to touch and taste
Enjoy this night I aim to please

Let my face meet your place
Cum on girl let my tongue be your guide
While I take you on this erotic ride

Let down your guard
I'm going to blow your mind
You will never experience anything like it

EVER.......

Love
NO LIMITS

We sex everywhere
No place is off limits
When my body is calling
You fulfill my needs
No matter where we are
You take me to ecstasy

The car who knew
The movies shh....
The beach black sands oh hell yeah
One place I never imagine
The elevator why not

I'm trying to stay quiet
So no one can hear
You make it so difficult
With every stroke you give
You have me begging for more

Just when I'm about to reach
The point of no return
The elevator starts moving
We must now hide our deed
For no one could ever know or have seen
How naughty and freaky we can be

Love

WET AND READY

Love I'm here wet and ready
Are you willing to make it sexy
Hot and Horny needing your love
Please give me what we both deserve

Your tongue is divine
Your lips so sweet
Baby please put them all over me

I'm ready for you to teach me
Show me how it's supposed to be done
I need you to make me cum and cum

Over and over
All in your mouth
Now isn't that what
Eating pussy is all about

Love

DEAREST

You listen to me
You understand what I mean
You are so attentive to me
We laugh we joke we can be seriously
But in the end you are my dearest
Dearest friend that's not so near
Giving me what I miss and need
Thank you for being you
So very kind
Your star shines bright
Thank you for your company
All those late nights we shared
So that I wouldn't be lonely
From the bottom of my heart
You're my one and only
Remember me always
For I will remember you
The one who got me through
A rough time in my life
I will cherish those moments forever
This I do swear Thank you oh thank you
Because I will always care

Love

BE

What is this that I'm doing
Not sure but it feels good
In just a short time how is it possible you bring out the smile
The smile I forgot I had

Trying so hard not to show I'm not happy where I am
Pretending to be when I know I can't
Not getting what I need from the one I'm with
Getting too much from the one I can't have

Such a burden to bare
In such despair
My heart ache and is pain
Pain that I wish would fade away

I love you but you're not the person you used to be
I'm falling in love with you but don't know if you are right for me
Must make a choice not easy to decide
Whatever it may be
It must be right

Don't want to hurt no one at all
No way for that not to happen
Wish there was another way
I made my choice
I cannot stay

This love thing we had is no longer there
Just only in my heart lock away
I can't live this life another day
I wish you the best she is waiting for me
I'm going to her cause that's where I want to be

Love

UTOPIA

Ignite my senses

Go ahead and listen

To my lyrics

While we both flow like a stream

Me with my words

You with your cream

Feeling like how could this be

Words stirred so intensely

Flicking my tongue

Putting it where it belongs

Saying things you can't believe

Never again will you under estimate me

Making you feel like a woman should be

And this is only the beginning

Welcome my Nubian Queen

To Utopia and it's not a dream....

Love

LOVE

The beginning of life lies within this flower
The POWER it holds
The Passion it gives
Touch Taste or Inside
It's Magical Palace
Safe is what you'll be
Never wanting to leave
Giving you all sorts of feelings
Mad, Love, Anger, Lust
Happiness, Pleasure, Distrust
A flower that can only be described
As intoxicating and toxic all at the same time
But no matter how you flip it
The shit is addictive
A flower like no other
What do we call her
~~~~ PUSSY ~~~~
And we must take care of her!

Love

ADDICTED

Please be sure
For once you begin
You will never want it to end
Exhilarating

Breathless is what you will become
For it will be I that takes it away
Feel me in your depth
That is beyond your soul
My presence will forever remain there

Forget me not
I'm that thing you can't do without
Addictive I am
Hell I've hooked lots of them

Once you've had me
This is how it will always be
You can never go free
I'm that one and only

A force so deep
It will have you guessing
But the injection you get
Will answer all those questions

Yes, you're addicted
Addicted to me
I told you already
In the very beginning

But I guess you just wasn't listening

Love

THAT GOOD

The forbidden fruit
Bearer of life
Sweet as it is poison

Nurturing as it is deadly
The beginning for all
The end for many

An illusion it seems to be
Not wanting to accept its trickery
But don't get it twisted

We all long to be in it
That's if you love the taste of its fruit
I know I do

Despite the hurt and pain
From being bitten
No other place I'll rather be
Than within it

Comforting soothing tranquility
Looking beyond the danger
That's right in front of me

I was lured by the aroma
Took a bite
Now my eyes are wide open

Good and Evil twisted as one
Can't undo what has been done
Accept my fate
For it has become my Destiny....

Love

REALITY

How can you turn off desire
When it lives within you
A burning fire
That only one can subdue
The pain of walking alone
With no one as your guide
Holding out from others
Waiting on that one true
But the truth is she's not there for you
Long gone into another
You wait patiently for your love to arrive
Only to realize you've been wasting your time
Time to move on
Find someone new
Because the reality is
She doesn't and never has loved you!

Love

FEEL ME

Do you feel my depth
Do you hear my whispers
Can you touch my soul
I long for you
Cry out your name
While I wait patiently for you to arrive
Which only seems in vain
As you don't see me
Invisible in your world
How I wish I could reach you
But you're so far away
Preoccupied with others
While I sit and suffer
Waiting for you to realize
I am the one
I have always been the only one
That can give you what you seek
But only if you let me

Love

DESTINY

I want to be a part of you
In a way that you have never experienced
Pick a part your most beautiful feature
Get inside the depths of your being
Touch you with my song that sings
Breathe life into your womb
Create something from you and me
Watch it grow daily
I will treat you like the QUEEN you were born to be
Do you trust me?
To open you up to all possible things
Wonders like you've never seen
I prayed for you and now you're here
To start that life we both have dreamed
I am your wife as you are mine
Walking a journey for just us two
Until the day when my light becomes dim
I'll close my eyes and wait for you once again!

Love

MY BLESSING MY CURSE

What's in my heart
Flows through my fingertips
Not what's seen through my eyes
Analyzed by my brain
But what flows NATURALLY
Uninhibited, Raw, Naked & Real
Always a blessing
Sometimes my curse
Swirling Dancing Running Skipping
Throughout my head
Words phrases
That turn into sentences
Which evolves into paragraphs
That create chapters
My life this is
Which I embrace
My creativity
I share with the world
Welcome to my chaos
The life of what
I cannot say
Just a woman with a pen
With endless writings
Sleepless nights
Wakes me up often
My characters talking
I wouldn't have it any other way
For this is my world
My saving grace
A pen and paper
On to it I scribble

Acknowledgments

First, I want to give honor to the Creator as I am nothing without you and everything with you! Thank you for the strengthen you have blessed me with. I want to thank Deborah Webster for her undying support and encouragement as both a friend and a partner! It is such a wonder thing to have someone in your corner who supports and loves you unconditionally, I love you always. To my cheering section by way of my daughters thank you for keeping me grounded. It's the love I have for you both that guides my life! To my nephew continue to make me proud I love you dearly. To every one of my supporters from the bottom of my heart I thank you for believing and rocking with me. Thank you all for supporting my dreams!

Forever always Unique Waterfall....

www.ingramcontent.com/pod-product-compliance
Lightning Source LLC
LaVergne TN
LVHW021548080426
835509LV00019B/2896